Jean Gerson

Practical Guide to Spiritual Prayer

Jean Gerson, H. Austin

Practical Guide to Spiritual Prayer

ISBN/EAN: 9783337959470

Printed in Europe, USA, Canada, Australia, Japan

Cover: Foto ©Lupo / pixelio.de

More available books at **www.hansebooks.com**

Practical Guide

to

SPIRITUAL PRAYER.

BY

JOHN GERSON.

LITERALLY TRANSLATED

BY THE REV. H. AUSTIN.

London:
THOMAS RICHARDSON AND SON,
23, KING EDWARD STREET, CITY;
AND DERBY.
1884.

PREFACE.

John Charlier, surnamed Gerson, took this name from a village in the diocese of Rheims, where he was born in 1363. He studied theology under Pierre d'Ailli, and succeeded him in the dignity of Chancellor and Canon of the Church of Paris. Some authors have attributed to him the excellent book of the "Imitation of Christ." He died in a Monastery of the Celestines, near Lyons, in France, in 1429.

The style of Gerson is said to be full of matter, soundly reasoned, but without polish.

𝔓ractical 𝔊uide

TO

SPIRITUAL PRAYER.

CHAPTER I.

THE DIVINE VOCATION.

God calls all men to salvation; for, according to the Apostle, God wills all men to be saved. It is from this that all have that natural craving for beatitude, which cannot be got rid of. Still, in the matter of divine vocation, one goes after this manner, another after that, according to the division of graces, administrations, and operations. For the Apostle says; "To one is given, by the Spirit, the word of wisdom, to another the word of knowledge, to another faith, to another the grace of healing, to another the working of miracles, to another prophecy, to another the discernment of spirits, to another the gift of tongues, to another the interpretation of speeches. But

all these worketh one and the same Spirit,
dividing to every one according as He will :
even as the body is one, and its members
have different offices."

Now, here it is said that the word of wisdom, which is very like the grace of contemplation, if it be not the very same thing, is
given by the Spirit, not to all, but to this
one or that one; just as is also the grace of
healing, faith, that is, (I fancy) peace in be-
lieving, working of miracles, prophecy, &c.,
&c. Just, then, as it is not fitting that all who
are called to glory should endeavour indis-
criminately to obtain some grace of adminis-
tration or operation, so neither ought all to
give themselves up to the pursuit of wisdom
or contemplation. In matters of the arts and
sciences the ancient philosophers have pointed
this out to those concerned in government of
states, for all cannot do all things. This is
too plain to require curious investigation.

Vocations being so various, and the settle-
ment often a matter of great difficulty, one
thinking himself called to this work, another
to that, each should strive to make sure his
calling to salvation. It is no small help to

this end to take counsel of experienced and
spiritual men, such as judge all things. The
consideration, too, of our own personal circumstances, and of our bodily temperament,
may assist us, our condition in life, our character, intellect, and temper.

Even of those called to contemplation all
are not at once able to be borne aloft into God.
Fearful and anxious, they look on Him as a
most severe judge, as an austere master,
whose condemnation once past knows no recal.
These in their groanings complain to God :
" Who knoweth the power of Thine anger,
and for Thy fear can number Thy wrath?"
Or again, " If Thou shalt mark iniquities, O
Lord, who shall stand?" Or again, " Enter
not into judgment with Thy servant, O Lord,
for in Thy sight shall no man living be justified." Or, " Rebuke me not, O Lord, in Thy
fury." This class do not so much desire the
eternal reward as they wish to escape eternal
punishment, which even the perfect may cau-
tiously fear. A second class are called hire-
lings, seeking a recompense from God for
their service, as from a most liberal king, or
as from the Father of mercies and God of all

consolation. These say with the prodigal: " Father, I have sinned against heaven and before Thee, and am no more worthy to be called Thy son; make me as one of Thy hired servants." These rightly behave as sons, but sons conscious of having done evil, and they do not reach so far as the perfect.

There are a third class, fewer in number, who do not seek God in a servile manner, nor after the manner of a hireling. Forgetful of their servitude, and of their reward, forgetful of God's paternal authority, they with more than filial mind consort with God as a friend with a friend; nay, they are knit to Him with a sweeter intimacy still, as a bride with her bridegroom, and their words are, " I to my Beloved, and His turning is towards me." Or again, " What have I in heaven ?" that is, for reward ; " and besides Thee what do I desire upon earth ?" that is, for the escaping of punishment. " For Thee my flesh and my heart hath fainted away. Thou art the God of my heart, and the God that is my portion for ever."

The first are the beginners, the second those that advance, the rest are the perfect. But all at times should treat with God as with a most severe judge, or again, as with a Master and Lord, a Father who keeps them, but will avenge every negligence; otherwise let them fear what is said, "Unless thou hold thyself constant in the fear of God, thy house will be speedily overturned."

But even after offences and adulteries we may return to our Spouse, for God says in Jeremias, "Thou hast committed fornication with many lovers, yet return to Me, and I will receive thee." Now, for the best manner of approaching God each one is at liberty to form his own judgment; but to my mind, the most advisable mode for most, is to go to Him as our Father who is in heaven. This induces a reverential fear and a childlike love, and it brings a person to ask with respectful confidence all things necessary for our toilsome pilgrimage. If we come before God as Lord, our judge, as the just one who speedily requites with vengeance, and the like, these names fill the soul with fear rather than with love. But, on the contrary, such names as spouse, love, abiding in delights and in beds of aromatical spices, my Beloved white and

ruddy, abiding between the breasts, whose
left hand is under my head, and His right
hand shall embrace me; these with some
breathe more of softness than of affection, and
procure less of sincere love. The name our
Father is in a wonderful manner between
both, so as to mix fear with love, and temper
love with fear.

CHAPTER II.

THE TEMPERAMENT.

It is a dictum of philosophers that the soul
follows the body, and we know this well by
daily experience. This following, however,
is not of necessity, either from within or from
without, but it is one of inclination. When a
work is in conformity with our natural bent,
this is a most wonderful help to its perform-
ance. When it is repugnant it is a great
hindrance. Our will, though free, though
schooled, though aided by custom, will scarcely
suffice to overcome the repugnance.

S. Gregory, so long and thoroughly versed
in the art of contemplation, tells us that he
had found some men so restless and fond of
change, that the quiet of contemplation was to
them, if not intolerable, at least most exceedingly irksome, whereas, others of a calmer
nature were most apt for it, and inclined that
way. To the first he allots the active life,
the second he sends to contemplation.

Now we all know that some men are more
passionate than others; some again have
great good sense and understanding; others
are mostly affectionate. It is by this that we
see some men arrive at compunction, and con-
sequently at the grace of contemplation, by
the passion of anger, through detesting the
vileness of their vices. The second set reach
contemplation more from a good judgment,
which loves truth, and sees how right and
beautiful it is to live in accordance with reason.
But one with a soft and friendly heart, easily
capable of compassion and love, such an one
as the spouse is described, whose soul melted
when her Beloved spoke, the all-desirable,—
one like this is drawn to the rest of contemplation by brooding over the Passion of our

Lord, or by considering the great condescension and love of God, or by something pious and touching in the lives of the Saints. Women, who are called the devout female sex, are often of this last character.

The cause, then, is plain why different ones are drawn rather by this than by that mode to contemplation ; for the mode of action suits their natural bent, and the flesh obeys the spirit more willingly in its upward flight, when it has in itself some concordance, or aptitude for that to which it is carried. Now, as far as we may conjecture from their deeds, it would appear that in S. Jerome and S. Ambrose the dominant principle in the temperament was that of anger, in S. Gregory and S. Bernard that of love and affection, but in S. Augustine and S. Thomas sound reason and intelligence. This, however, does not exclude from any of them the loving and friendly heart capable of deep affection, nor does it exclude from each a searching study after truth, and a vehement zeal against all that is unseemly in conduct.

How thankful ought those to be who are well born, whether, like John Baptist, they owe this to a miracle of God's hand, or they have it flow to them from their ancestors and parental stock, or they have been carefully brought up in good and wholesome morality; this grace, from whatever source it come, let them not receive it in vain. Let each take care, says S. Bernard, that the word which cometh forth from the mouth of the Lord shall not return to Him vain, but shall prosper, and do all things for which God sent it, so that each may say, The grace of God in me was not in vain. To neglect the gift is an injury to the giver. Not to use it is a token of intolerable pride, and hateful thanklessness of heart.

CHAPTER III.

THE PERSONAL CONDITION.

How vast is the variety of ranks and occupations in the world! In the world, as in the Church, all the members have not the same office. But the call to contemplation requires leisure from outward cares; and as many are bound, by their office and state of life, to be in busy exercise and bustle, both for mind and body, how can a counsel to contemplation be given to such? They would simply spoil both. "*The enemy shall behold them, and shall mock at their Sabbaths.*" (Lam. i. 7.)

We may, then, pass in silence those who are occupied in mechanical works, shops, and hard country labour; those again in bonds of marriage, when the woman has thoughts of the world, how she may please her husband, and the man to provide for his wife and children. Prelates, says S. Gregory, ought to be, above all others, lost in contemplation. But if they then first want to study contemplation, when they ought to be attending to the wants of their subjects, they deceive themselves. In abandoning the care of their people for the sweets of contemplation they give way to a temptation, for they neglect a necessary obligation to attend to a thing of their own will, not necessary.

Where, however, contemplation has become a familiar thing, and a man can use both hands, and so, like an angel of God, can con-

template in the midst of action, or can immediately after action betake himself to
contemplation without much difficulty, then
it is right enough, and just suits the state of
contemplation in exercise to which he is
called.

The ecclesiastical state, especially in those
who are Religious, is to tend to this perfection,
and for this purpose they are set in the school
of prayer and devotion, that they may be like
the eyes of the Church, making the other
members attend to God and to themselves.

Children are little capable of contemplation;
but looking to the future, great care must be
taken that their young minds get no taint by
foul words, or pictures, or things. Everything
that is modest and religious they should be
imbued with. A new vessel once defiled re-
tains the evil savour long after. Our Lord,
therefore, denounced a woe on those who
scandalized His little ones. Youths ought to
be more burdened with bodily exercises to
repress the violence of their passions. When
these are moderated by age and custom, the
remainder of life may be given all to the quiet
of contemplation.

CHAPTER IV.

AIMING AT PERFECTION.

Many say, "The common life is enough for me. If I can be saved with the lowest, that will suffice; I have no wish for the merits of the Apostles; I do not want to soar aloft, I am content to go on the level." Such as these should consider that this imperfection is a refusal to be perfect; for in the way of God not to advance is to go back. The slothful servant is condemned, because, being content to keep his talent, he did not give it out to interest. This may be made clear by an example.

Supposing some great gentleman has several children, capable by their talents of greatly increasing his wealth and consideration; but one of them, whilst the rest enter this or that profession, and make their way in life, stops at home idle, doing nothing suitable to his talents or to his noble birth, but saying that he is quite content to remain as he is, provided he does nothing particularly disgraceful. In this case, if, when the father calls on his son, and spurs him to do something more noble, yet the son turns a deaf ear, and obeys not his wishes, will not such a son become hateful to his father? Now, those put themselves in this very position with our heavenly Father whom He draws to more excellent graces and diviner actions; but they are dull, sticking in the mud, and making no effort after perfection.

Those that are tied by some office, or by their state of life, cannot, without transgressing a precept, rise to these higher things, and what has been said does not speak of them: their highest merit is to work in obedience to the divine command. Mary, too, might honourably with Martha have ministered to our Lord as her guest; yet she is praised because, intent on one thing, she chose the best part. He then is to be blamed who makes the worser part his.

From what has been said it plainly follows that since the contemplative life is more perfect, according to theologians, than the active, he who is suited for it, and is not tied by

necessity to action, is at perfect liberty to give
up the active life to embrace contemplation.
S. Augustine says that, if no work of charity
is imposed on us, *i.e.*, by necessity or a
superior's injunction, we should study to con-
template truth.   Nor need any one fear to be
condemned as having hidden his talent, on
which he could have traded by preaching,
serving the poor, and other works of the active
life; for a contemplative person with heart
and eye, is of plentiful profit to the Church,
devoutly serving God, whilst others minister
with the mouth, the hands, or the feet.

The neglect of contemplation is very blame-
able in those who are placed in the school of
the Religious life, as a school of prayer, devotion, and tears; so also with such priests as
have plenty to live on and little to do.   Many
secular persons also, men and women, have
sufficient leisure, instruction, and abilities, to
give themselves thus wholly to God.   Filled
with faith, hope, and charity, they would
require little instruction to pass wholly to
a good state of heart.

CHAPTER V.

THE AVOIDANCE OF OCCUPATIONS.

The wise man says, " Write wisdom in the time of leisure, for he that is less in action shall perceive her." Let thy actions, then, be few, if thou wouldst be of good mind. No one, it is said, full of occupation finds wisdom. The perfect, even in occupation have wisdom, but they found it in leisure. A bird that has its wings tied, or daubed with lime, cannot fly upwards; a man who has his feet bound cannot swim; so a man full of occupation cannot soar into the heights of contemplation. For this there is required a wide vacuum; the heart must be like a blank sheet, not filled with cares, straitened with anxieties, or befouled with filthy passions, or there will be no place for the writing of the immense doctrine of wisdom.

What happens with trees will give us an example; if there is a wound in the bark, the sap that should ascend to nourish the tree, in-

stead of this flows out by the wound, and is
wasted idly on the ground. Now love is fitly
called the sap of the soul: the wounds of the
soul are fleshly passions, earthly cares and
the like; when there is this wound, love, instead of going upwards as a nutriment to
heavenly desires, flows downwards and is lost.
Those who would fain poise their wings and
soar aloft in the flights of contemplation,
grieve often to find that the sap of their love
is running downwards to the wounded place of
their hearts, to temporal cares, to a thought
of anger, to some anxiety, or the like. They
experience what the prophet bewails, when
he says : " My loins, *i.e.*, my affections, are
filled with illusions." *(Ps.* l.) These are the
illusions which he elsewhere calls " vanities
and false madnesses." This made the poet
say :

"Would'st thou be free from envy or evil love,
　Fill thee with good, and turn to the things above."

Is there any one, however, entirely free
from these troubles? No one: for all is
vanity. It is one thing, however, to give
oneself up to these distracting thoughts,

whether by duty, or zeal for such occupations, and quite another to suffer them unwillingly, wiping them away, as it were, with the hand of discretion; driving them off as teasing flies; just as Abram kept off the birds that hovered over his evening sacrifice.

Now, as regards the occupation of many Religious in singing psalms and hymns with high sounding chants, multiplied beyond number; does this help them either to attain or to exercise contemplation? What is to be thought of it? It is true that S. Augustine wept plentifully, in hearing the sweet melody of the hymns of the Church, and was wonderfully moved by the voices, and the truth distilled into his heart; but it is not said that he was one of the singers. However, as grace will do more to bring a person to the quiet of contemplation than our own industry, and since there are intermissions in the singing, it is quite possible that some persons with their minds thus engaged have had raptures, especially in cases where the person was striving to rise from the sensual to the rational, or further still to the spiritual man.

It may be, too, that this multiplication of psalm-singing has been ordained more for the sake of the sensual, that is, to occupy the minds of such as know not how to meditate in quiet with themselves, or to make good use of their leisure, than for spiritual persons, who are rare. Indeed a well ordered Institute might, perhaps, make such more free from this yoke, so as to have some at least with Mary sitting at the feet of Jesus, and not to have only Martha.

If whilst singing psalms, God and His Spirit visits the soul, nothing is mightier or more blessed. Blessed, says David, is the the people that knoweth jubilation, singing wisely, and joining to the words the understanding and affections. Happy indeed is such a soul. For such an one, O my Jesus, is not like land without water to Thee, but she is Thy love, Thy dove, Thy spouse. For in saying the hours she fulfils the precept of religious praise, yet is privileged like one in deepest solitude, and is still more mighty, still more blessed than such.

It is good by premeditation to make ready matter for the time of prayer, that the affections may be more speedily enkindled.

It is good, too, from what is said, not to seek a subtle and manifold knowledge, so much as relish and exultation. For often where there is less knowledge there is more affection, and love enters when knowledge stands without. We should imitate those who rejoice at the sound of the drum and the harp, who feel delighted enough with the melody, without examining over nicely about the rules of harmony.

All then that we hear read, or think, should be drawn to good affections. If we hear Pater noster, our mind should rise to reverence and love, to beg for our necessities and those of others, of whom God is the common Father. Then, in considering who is our Father, we should have noble thoughts, and despise all that is low and foul; unsuited with the royalty of our extraction. And as our Father is in heaven, we should mourn our exile on the the earth, far from our true inheritance.

Such affections as these can be found without end or number; sweet and new every day, hidden as honey in the comb; or as manna flowing abundantly, when pressed by the teeth of contemplation.

CHAPTER VI.

WITHDRAWAL OF CONTEMPLATION.

In following contemplation it must not be from curiosity. Curiosity is either a study about unprofitable things, or a searching into those that are profitable, beyond what is lawful, becoming, or expedient. We should not sigh after contemplation to get knowledge of its lofty heights, as scanned by the Saints, nor with the purpose of making them known presently to others. Our object should rather be that we may be viler in our own eyes, our vileness being seen the more clearly by the comparison of the contemplation of the Godhead; or that we may be stronger against temptation, more fervent in the love of God and of our neighbour, and stricter in the keeping of God's commandments.

We ought also to tremble when we consider that there are faithless children, and wicked servants; to whom, nevertheless, the heavenly Father sometimes gives of the fat of wheat, and satiates them with honey out of the rock; just indeed as some princes have to persons condemned to death, sent, shortly before their execution, dainties from their own table. We must not then be over wise, but fear, since the grace of contemplation is reckoned amongst the graces *gratis datæ;* which, like faith, and hope, and prophecy, and other powers, may be had lifeless, and without charity. No one securely glories, but he who glories in the Lord.

Woe, then, to human presumption, for these and the like spiritual gifts are to be found sometimes with the cursed and reprobate children, either to the increase of their damnation by their most ungrateful use of the gift of God; or for the instruction of others; or as a sort of transitory reward for their labours as false and unprofitable. Like labour, like reward, says the proverb. They desired in a manner to commit fornication with the gifts of God, by a wicked love, of presumption, and what then? God gave them the desire of their hearts, but in anger. So they hear the Gospel,—Take that is thine, and go thy way.

2

Now God, by a merciful dispensation, often withdraws from His elect, but not in wrath nor to the end; but who shall be able to sound the deep abyss of His judgments? We may, from the sayings of the Saints, who have some of them spoken of these mysteries, learn something, God having inspired them to speak. This happens, then, often for our humiliation, either to check pride that has arisen, or to prevent it from rising. S. Bernard therefore testifies that nothing so powerfully helps either to find, keep, or recover this grace, as not to be too loftily wise, but to be wise unto sobriety. Blessed is the man that is always fearful, and stands upon his watch.

Sometimes, again, God does this to inflame the desire more vehemently, as a fire pent up rages afterwards more fiercely. God would have us seek great things in a grand manner.

This happens that man's fragility, and the depth of his miseries, may be seen by him more clearly, so that he may grow vile in his own eyes, considering what he is in himself, and what by the grace of God he can be.

Sometimes it is done to teach pity for those in desolation, to whom comfort is not given;

or, after being given, is taken away. It takes place that a man may satisfy either for himself or others, by the painful sense of abandonment, just as our Lord's human nature was abandoned and steeped in a torrent of pains, that so He might satisfy, not for His own sins, but those of others.

It may be also, because one who is capable by his learning of assisting others, wills ever to be at leisure for himself, and loving the embraces of Rachel, refuses the work of charity, has no care to give fruitfulness to Lia. But a well ordered nature has a horror of idleness; so when it finds it cannot rise to high things, it seeks occupation in those that are lower. Thus this soul made weak and humbled, is thereby perfected more completely, and receives the willing showers of divine dew.

Again, this happens, that being tempted in many things, a man may learn obedience and other virtues, so as to teach them with greater power. For that saying of Socrates is true, we speak best of what we know best. That we know best, which we have had intimate

experience of; the inexperienced man, what
does he know?

God takes away contemplation, lest on its
account man should neglect the obligation of
the divine commands.

Sometimes He punishes venial defects this
way, just as an indulgent father might turn
away his face from a wanton son; or show a
sad look, that his son might be more careful
in future in keeping himself strictly modest,
and lest, by neglecting small things, he might
fall by little and little.

It happens again, that we may know how
true that word of the Apostle is: "It is not
of him that willeth, nor of him that runneth,
but of God, who showeth mercy." For it is
not by our own industry that we arrive at
contemplation. And this becomes a plain
sign, since after a man has said to himself
that at such a time he will be free, and will
prepare himself for the enjoyment of the
sweets of contemplation, lo, when the time
comes, he finds himself dry, and filled with
bitterness; no relish for reading, or prayer,
only darkness and trouble. On the contrary,
when we are not expecting it, and have pre-

pared nothing, God visits us with the longed-for grace.

Sometimes it is done to purify the spiritual sea, a sea great and wide; for this sea, like the material sea, contracts filth by too long a quiet, and agitation and commotion clear it away.

Sometimes God thus proves whether the soul is ready to serve Him at her own cost, in pains and tribulation, with no salary of consolations and sweetness. For some there are who refuse to pray, or who imagine their prayer to be useless, if they do not receive a comfort with it, as if God never gave a precept of labour.

God at times weans us, to make the virtue of hope necessary, or lest we should make these consolations a sort of last end, or should receive our reward here below instead of looking for one to come. Just so sometimes a prince does not at once recompense a brave soldier, or a father his son, having in his mind some very great reward. Still, usually smaller gifts are at once bestowed, whilst the more solid marks of love are reserved for the future.

Sometimes so great a Guest declines to come to the soul, lest His coming should put her to too great expense, just as David refused the invitation of his son Absalom. But what are the expenses? Sighs and tears of contrition, fasting, and short sleep, which burden the body. Or it may be the soul is too young, and cannot yet bear too much of the intoxicating draughts of the Spirit, if the King were to bring her into the cellars of wine. So He keeps the key in His own hand, now opening and now shutting as He will.

Again, God so acts as the eagle provoking its young to fly, or as a mother teaching her child to walk. A mother sometimes hides herself from her child, that her child as forsaken may cry for her, and that when she returns he may be more cautious to stick close to her, that he may take greater care not to fall, that he may rejoice at having found her, and that sweetness may be added to her kisses and caresses.

God does it for the exercise of patience, because patience hath a perfect work; for what tribulation is more bitter, and what more plentiful material of patience can there be than for a soul that was having a foretaste of the delights of paradise, to fall, as it were, into the pains of hell, the likeness of the shadow of death, the miseries of the exile? Some conjecture may be formed, by the grief it suffers, of the bitterness of an eternal separation.

Now those who would devote themselves to contemplation should do so with all their force, yet still expect the result from above. They must be prepared to accept of it thankfully, and use it humbly when given, and when denied, to be still of good heart. They must love those who have this grace, and not despise those who have it not, remembering always that the kingdom of God consists only in loving God.

But the spiritual as well as the natural earth is subject to the curse. It does not bring forth its fruits without thorns and thistles. The soul does not bring forth her offspring of truth without pain.

CHAPTER VII.

THE NEED OF PATIENCE.

Now it may chance that, from the consideration of what has gone before, some may be
tempted to set aside all endeavours to obtain
the sweet and wholesome fruits of contemplation, saying, " Why should I labour in
vain, why strive to get what may not be profitable to my soul, what may be obtained only
to my condemnation? Let the holy will of
God be done. If He wills it, let Him give
me here a foretaste of His sweetness, and if
He wills, let Him deny it; my heart is ready
for both."

But you who would thus talk should know
that though he who plants is nothing, nor he
who waters, yet God wills that we shall both
plant and water diligently, whether in the
natural or spiritual order.   Otherwise how
can we be " fellow helpers with God"?   And
if we give up our own efforts, looking to the
divine help alone, how do we fulfil the saying,

"Thou shalt not tempt the Lord thy God"? Let us, then, do our part, our industry, planting and watering, and let Christ give the increase by a quickening virtue poured from above. From Him we must seek it in lowly confidence.

Let no one excuse himself from aiming at contemplation, kept back by negligence and a sluggish heart. The consideration telling us to tend to perfection should shame such. And let no one give up the journey to perfection because he finds snares and temptations laid in the pathways. Even if often driven back, and seeming to make no progress, let him still press on. But let him lean not on the reed of his own efforts, but on the strong staff of the protection of God Most High.

He that receiveth it, let him receive it. For the grace of contemplation is to be sought by labour, and labour is required to obtain that which it cannot give. But so we see in the formation of man. The generation comes from the father, the nourishing in the womb from the mother, and without these how could a child be born? Still, all would be to no purpose unless God gave the soul from above.

By the sole will of the Creator is the life
given, without which all would be without
form and unprofitable.

A man removes the shutters, raises his
head, opens his eyes. How without this can
he see? But with all this, if the sun with-
held its beams all would be in vain. It is the
same with the Sun of Justice. If God gives
nothing to men without great labour, as an
ancient author says; if no one is crowned unless he strives lawfully, as the apostle de-
clares; if again the learning of minor things
costs such care and trouble, to escape poverty,
to increase wealth, to get honour or some
perishable good, and labour overcomes all
difficulties,—" labor omnia vincit,"—then
surely we ought to blush with shame to be
less careful, patient, and energetic in our
search for this most beautiful and excellent
divine grace of contemplation.

The brave pilgrim that would ascend this
mount of contemplation must go forth strenu-
ously like a giant to run his course. He must
plant his foot firmly, so as not to slip back-
ward. And if he should slip, he must rise
again with vigour, shaking from off his neck

the burden of earthly thoughts. He should do as did the fabled Sisyphus. How long shall we be content to lie in the valley of tears, in the deep mire and mud? Let us sigh for the peace and joy of the Spirit in a purer atmosphere.

CHAPTER VIII.

ROOTS OF THE PASSIONS.

Mystical theology has this peculiarity, that whereas all other sciences have their seat in the understanding, this has its seat in the affections. And as every affection is either itself love, or takes its rise from love, mystical theology may be fitly termed the art of love, the science of loving. Love is so surely the source of all the other affections and passions, that even hatred is born of love. In a confused manner all are in love. Hope and fear, joy and sorrow, equally spring from love.

If God is loved above all things, then that which opposes Him is hated. Again, as the soul recognises in God an object of sovereign delight, joy is felt at His presence, sorrow or fear at His absence. Authors disagree as to the number of the passions, some enumerating more, others fewer. Hugh of S. Victor counts nine, though he hints that the passions are innumerable. However, three may be considered enough, corresponding to the power, wisdom, and goodness of God. Suitably with this division, Richard of S. Victor divides the graces of contemplation, according to the triple exclamation concerning the devout soul in the Canticles: where she is likened, from her abundance of compunction, to a pillar of smoke; and from the greatness of her admiration to the morning rising; and from the fulness of her joy, to one leaning on her beloved.

If, then, we consider deeply the riches and power of God, and our own poverty and frailty, how can we help being pierced with dread, thinking on our own wretched unworthiness, and shuddering, because we have sinned against a Judge who is so terrible in His counsels over the sons of men, against so powerful a Lord, so majestic a Father.

Again, if we consider with the eyes of our mind how wonderful is God's knowledge, so high that we cannot reach to it, our minds fail with wonder and amazement; for it can in no wise take in how it is that some are destined by Him for glory, and some He foreknows will go into everlasting misery. We cannot understand how it is that He denies many things to those who are thankful, and would use them well, and yet gives them to the ungrateful, who then fight against Him. Or again, how for almost their whole life He endures some who are sunk in abominable crimes, and saves them like the thief on the Cross, whilst upon others, who, like Judas, are to perish everlastingly, He bestows the grace of divers virtues.

How stupefying it is to consider that no one can correct that man whom He despises, that He hath shut up all under sin, and the like. The sight of these things forced from the Apostle that bewildered exclamation, " O, the height and the depth of the riches, the wisdom, and knowledge of God," &c.

But last there comes into the mind the thought of the torrent of divine sweetness, and

3

how good God is to Israel; to those of an
upright heart. Then, full of exultation, the
soul cries out: How sweet, O Lord, is Thy
Spirit. How great is the multitude of Thy
sweetness, which Thou hast laid up for them
that fear Thee.

We have, then, here the three principal
affections; compunction with fear, admiration
with amazement, and exultation with glad-
ness, exercised in reference to the power,
wisdom, and goodness of God, and according
to the three powers of the soul as defined by
the school-men; the irascible, the rational,
and the concupiscible.

Again, nothing will be found in the whole
of Scripture, which by this recognition may
not be fitted to a prayer that shall appease
God. The power of God may be opposed to
our own weakness, and to the tyranny of our
foes; God's wisdom to our folly and the craft
of our enemies; God's benevolence against our
malice and that of others. Every thing we
read in Scripture, and indeed all we see, seems
to be speaking to us of our misery, the wicked-
ness of our enemies, or the majesty of God, in
power, wisdom, and goodness.

But if our thoughts are vain and earthly, if the spring of love be corrupted, then passions of a similar kind will rise up, but perverse and froward. Vain fear will rise from the dread of poverty, or of death by the violence of some tyrant; an unprofitable compunction. Admiration will enjoy the sight of deceitful cunning; whilst from filthy pleasure, false joy will spring, and from the worst of things a still baser glorying.

To have, then, our affections praiseworthy, there must be a pure spring of love to make them grow, and the honest and good ground of a true faith and of holy thought must drink in the watering of the spring. Hence the Apostle warns us to have our minds reformed and purged, that is, from the fever of a corrupt love, so that our eyes may look to that which is alone supremely fair and full of light, our ears may drink in true harmony of sound, our taste may savour the highest sweetness, our smell the most exquisite perfumes, and our touch what is most pleasant and delightful, all the senses being lifted up into God.

We may consider the affections and passions in another manner, as affected from without and from within, through the fancy, imagination or reason, through illuminations from God and good Angels, through bad angels, against whom we have to fight rather than against flesh and blood, so that the most pure and holy souls are sometimes forced to suffer the troublesome stings of blasphemous and most filthy thoughts. Sometimes in old age and solitude, they feel tempted in a sort that they never were when young, and in the midst of the snares of the world.

We may again, conformably with the teaching of Aristotle in his rhetoric, consider the natural causes and roots of the passions, whence modesty comes, whence vain-glory, whence shame, despair, amazement, admiration, anger, envy, &c., whence comes the appetite for flattering, for detraction, reverence, detestation, and the four general passions of hope, fear, sorrow, and joy.

S. Augustine, that most subtle analyser of the thoughts, says, that in every vice we are really wishing to imitate in some way the excellence of God; so true it is that the beginning of every sin is pride. What is sin but an unmeasured inordinate affection. Pride, then, is the root of every froward affection ; and, on the contrary, humility is the mother of every pious affection. The shortest and most incisive rule, then, for discerning between good and bad affections, is this double root, one of which will manifest its flavour in the fruits of the affection if tasted carefully.

Is any one envious ? it is because he desires that he alone should excel. Is he angry ? he wishes to excel undisturbed. Is he avaricious, he wishes to excel in being clear of want. Is he slothful ? he wishes to excel in freedom from toil. Is he lustful ? he wishes to excel in pleasure ; and so of gluttony. Is he fainthearted, arrogant, or disobedient ? Does he do ill for no reason, one would think ? it is to excel in his self-will, and to do all these things unpunished.

Take away this longing to excel unpunished, and immediately the branches, leaves, and fruits springing therefrom will wither away. Then, instead of envy, will come charity ; and instead of anger, meekness ; instead of avarice, liberality ; and instead of sloth, vigorous action, and so of the rest. In these the Man Christ is imitated ; in the others it is Lucifer.

CHAPTER IX.

THE TIME AND PLACE.

Some places are public, others private; some quiet, others noisy; some dark and small, others light and roomy, open to the air. So in time there is afternoon, and evening, and night, cock crowing, dawn, daylight, first, third, sixth, and ninth hours. There is again posture suitable for contemplation, standing, kneeling, lying flat. One will lie on his face, another on his back; again, one will place his face between his knees, another covers his with his hands, another leans on his elbow; one lifts his eyes upwards, another casts them down, another lets them wander hither and thither; one stands still, another walks about. Every one abounds in his own sense, according to the word of the Apostle.

The rule, then, in these matters is for every one to do what seems good in his own eyes to facilitate his contemplation, unless those who are tied by a common Religious discipline to a particular observance, either of time, or place, or posture. For woe to him that causes scandal by his singularity. For who hath devoured the vineyard of the Lord ? Truly a *singular wild beast* such as this. (Ps. lxxix.)

Some persons are helped by being in a low, narrow, dark place, silent, and fearful with horror. Such as these dwell, as it were, in tombs, hollow places of the earth, and caverns. Others like an open, large, and lightsome place, lofty, and with plenty of open air. These have dwelt in the mountains and in deserts, where S. Jerome says there is an indescribable serenity, quite different from the smoke of cities.

Some hate the slightest sound, but others do not mind it at all. The sound of water falling, or the whisper of the leaves, or the song of birds, or dashing of the waves on the sea shore, is a help to them. Some especially are assisted by church music, the voices in choir, or the bells or organ.

What incites others to wanton thoughts gives to some thoughts that are modest and grave. With some, though few, dances and harping, and the beauty of women in splendid array of gold and variety, are converted into high and truest contemplation and raptures, whilst to others these things minister only to silly and filthy lust. To those who so love God all things work together for good, so that they make profit out of everything, like bees collecting their honey. Those who are lifted up from the earth draw all things to themselves.

Now, what rule is to be laid down about the variety of times, since there is a time to laugh, and a time to weep, a time to embrace, and a time to refrain from embracing. Again, the Psalmist says, " Seven times a day will I praise Thee, because of the judgments of Thy justice." And in another place he says, " In the middle of the night did I rise to confess to Thee." And again he says, that in the morning he slew all the sinners of the earth; that is, he subjected all temptations to sin, which he could not have done but by watching and praying. Again, he says to the Lord, " Thou shalt make the outgoings of the morning and evening to be joyful." But who can dare to set God His time? Must we not rather watch and wait for the time of His own good pleasure? The afflicted Job says of man, " Thou visitest him early, and suddenly provest him."

However, in so far as respects our own efforts, perhaps the most fitting time for prayer is when our food is digested, and the cares of the world are laid aside, and when no one is present to observe us, when no one can mark our deep-drawn sighs, our sobs or groanings, our prostrations or weeping eyes, our cheeks now red, now pale, our uplifted hands, the beating of our breast, the kissing of the altar or the ground, and other suppliant gestures.

For bodily posture that is the best which helps the quiet of the mind. The prudent soul sits and is at rest. Nor can the mind be in peace unless the body has learned to remain fixed in the same posture.

For place, a holy one is ordinarily best, where there is the power of Christ's presence, the solemn consecration, where the prayers of the faithful are said, the deeds of the Saints are depicted, and where are the graves of the dead.

And who caħ doubt that at sacred and
solemn times a more plentiful river of divine
grace flows down, both on the living that are
sick, and the dead in the prison of purgation.
Then we come in a good day; then with more
confidence may we say to the Saints, " Be
favourable on this thy day of triumph." Then
more abundant remnants of graces fall like
crumbs for the poor from the magnificent
table of the blessed, to be given to those
beggars who ask, and seek, and knock.   Does
not the Church sing of Esther's wedding,
" This is the marriage of our human nature
with the Godhead ; on this day, through all
the world, the heavens are flowing with
honey" ?   As ordinary beggars, the sick and
halt, we should know how to choose our time,
or as prisoners who receive some better remnants of food from the table of their judge.

To speak now of the diversity of times.
There is a time to weep, and a time to laugh,
that is, a time of adversity, symbolised by
night in holy Scripture, and a time of prosperity, typified by the day.   To pass by the
perfect, who know how to make use of both
by the armour of justice on the right hand and

on the left, clever with both hands, and able to
say with the Apostle, "I know how to abound,
and how to suffer need, to rejoice with them
that rejoice, and to weep with them that
weep." With such that line of Virgil is true,

" Mens immota manet, lacrymæ volvuntur inanes."

For the mind remains fixed in the centre of
eternity, like an axle round which runs the
wheel of temporal things, or as a needle that
is magnetised turns to the pole.

Passing these by, it must be allowed, with
the Scripture, that for beginners and advancers
the time of adversity is most profitable, if the
adversity be moderate, and such as leaves un-
touched the judgment of reason, so that by the
gift of God patience brings forth fruit. For
adversity with a stronger hand warns them to
clear themselves out of the deep mire, and
lift themselves up from earth, since it is there
they find tribulation and sorrow. They therefore become more in earnest, and call on the
name of the Lord. For they know that God
is nigh to them that are of a troubled spirit,
and that He brings seasonable help in tribu-

lation, as it is written, " Call on Me in the
day of trouble, and thou shalt glorify Me."

Thus the rational dove, not finding where to
set the foot of its desire, returns to the ark of
contemplation, and as the waters of tribulation
increase, the ark is still higher lifted up.
Thus Anna and Peter ascended in trouble to
the upper parts of the house, being in dis-
grace, or afflicted by the death of relations,
the misfortunes of their country, or poverty.

This is a sort of spiritual *antiperistosis*,
which fortifies the contrary.* This is the
whetstone to sharpen the knife. This is the
wormwood that weans the infant from the
breast, the mallet that stretches the metal.
" In tribulation," says the Psalmist, " Thou
hast enlarged me." This is the file that
polishes, and takes off the rust, and brightens
up. This is the furnace that purges from the
dross. This is the rod that by striking delivers
from hell. He that suffers tribulation may
say with Ezekias, "Lord, if man's life be such,
and the life of my spirit be in such things as
these, Thou shalt correct me, and make me to

* An application of cold to increase heat, or heat
to increase cold.

live. Behold, in peace is my bitterness most bitter." Or again, " Let rottenness enter into my bones, and swarm under me, that I may rest in the day of tribulation, and mount up," that is, by contemplation, "to a girded people," that is to say, of the citizens above.

CHAPTER X.

FOOD AND SLEEP.

Now it is to be remarked, first, that a different observance is to be practised by beginners in contemplation from that of those who are making progress, and from that of the perfect. For the perfect have by custom their senses so exercised that, with the apostle, they know how to abound and how to suffer need, and in every place to lift up pure hands.

It is otherwise with beginners. They require props till a firmer building has been set up. The remarks about the observance of times and places apply to them as well as

these now on moderation in food and sleep.
As in beginning of contemplation very great
labour of mind is required, and this is a con-
siderable drain on the vital force, a corres-
pondent recovery is necessary, by means of
food and sleep, either taken in greater quantity at a time, or with more frequency.

But it may be said that a plentiful meal
burdens and clogs the soul. The taste of
fleshly things causes spiritual ones to lose
their relish. This may be true of a plentiful
meal, but not of a temperate one. But even
a plentiful meal, though it burden just a little
after taking, may still be esteemed temperate, if we look to the issue in the long run.
There have been persons, who, in order to get
the grace of contemplation, have copied the
austerity and abstinence of Elias, Daniel, and
John the Baptist, or the Fathers of the Desert;
but instead of prophets, they became mad-
men. Their example teaches that all cannot
fly with the perfect. Some graces are given
for admiration, not for imitation.

If the body is weakened, not only by fasts
and broken sleep, but by mental labour too,
and thus the vital force is exhausted, what can

we look for in such a case but a speedy dis-
solution, or grievous sickness, or a softening
of the brain ? The body, then, is to be helped
with food, not overwhelmed either by gluttony or famishment. But a hungry belly
that often wants food is better, according to
S. Jerome, than a two days fast.

If, then, one who is beginning contemplation is tied by Religious profession to obey
some indiscreet teacher, who will not let him
have enough food or sleep, it will be best for
him to moderate his exercise of meditation,
his contrition, and his tears, lest he should
lose himself, and become foolish, by the injury
of his reason. It must be enough for him just
to follow the community, if he would not
entirely bring his body to ruin.

It is well known, however, that the food
and sleep which is too little for one is too
much for another. It is impossible, then,
exactly to lay down a measure for all. Each
one's proper experience, well weighed, will
teach him the suitable quantity, or he may
trust himself to the counsel of the wise, or
the unction of the Spirit will guide him.
Medical doctors and theologians agree in this,

that indiscreet fasting is more hurtful than
intemperate eating; the latter can be reme-
died, but the former is often incurable; though
nature is content with little, if gluttony be
not yielded to.

We may take a lesson from what we see in
plants. Some are helped by plentiful and
frequent watering, others wither away under
the same treatment. Some grow and bear
fruit best, when planted by running water or
in marshy ground, others seek rather lofty
and dry ground, flourishing green on stony
gravel. Others again, when freshly planted,
require some moderate supply of water, till
they get well rooted; after, a very small
quantity suffices.

Now, the wise man says, "The body, which
is corrupted, weighs down the soul." This is
still more so, if gluttony, drunkenness, or
worldly cares are added. But as a superior
virtue, either of nature or good habits, or
fortified from above, can more easily bridle
and rule the lower powers, even though they
resist by their weight or corruption, so a
virtuous man, who has grown strong, either
through God's gift or by long exercise, is not

distracted by his body being loaded with food, or his mind with worldly cares, in the same way as one unpractised. One unpractised might have his reason overturned or greatly troubled, just as an unskilled sailor in a storm, when the ship rises now mountains high, and then sinks into an abyss, is utterly confused, whereas the pilot sticks firm by the wheel all the time, quite unmoved. In these matters, then, of eating and drinking, let that saying of the apostle be followed: "Let not him that eateth despise him that eateth;" and so of the rest of things, which vary according to varying circumstances.

CHAPTER XI.

SILENT MEDITATION.

Those who think to secure the grace of contemplation by assiduous reading, vocal prayers, or listening to devout discourses, deceive themselves. These things are helps, but do not of themselves suffice. It may be that, whilst reading or listening, a person may feel compunction; but take away the book or the sermon, and away goes the compunction with it. It is necessary, therefore, in silence to wait for God's salvation, and to get accustomed to pray with mind and spirit, without any sound of the voice, and without looking at a book. The meditation must be the book and the sermon, or the soul will never arrive at wisdom.

Some, however, complain that they cannot recollect themselves in silence. The mind flies off hither and thither, but a book or a sermon keeps it close tied. No doubt, to keep the spirit from wandering is a hard task, a difficult toil: but every effort must be made to secure this. We must sit solitary if we would raise ourselves above ourselves, so that we should not easily seek refuge from this in a book or a sermon.

But it will appear, perhaps, that we waste our time in this silence, and we are tired of it, as unprofitable. We must not be too hasty; silence will become less irksome by delay. To break it easily will render the practice still more wearisome. It may ease the mind for the while, but just as a dog, beaten away from a bone, returns to it, so will this cause the craving to break silence to be more severe. Alas! this is the reason why contemplative persons are so rare, even amongst those well read, priests, religious, and theologians; for we cannot arrive at contemplation unless by enduring to meditate long alone. Before the mind has scarce begun to meditate, some other thing is sought, reading, or conference, or the like, which hinder sin indeed, and give refreshment, on the plea of not wearying the soul in vain. This plea, however, is false, for if we only persevere seeking and knocking, God will not forget at length to be merciful to us.

Now, what meditations are fittest to excite good affections? It is impossible to say exactly. Many men, many minds. The kind of meditation must vary with each individual. Still we may specify some few out of many, calculated to excite holy fear.

It is truly and divinely said that the fear of the Lord is the beginning of wisdom. But to prevent fear from running to despair, we must ally hope with it. Fear is the beginning with almost all, as we see it was with S.

Bernard (super Cantica), and with Richard of
S. Victor, on the Twelve Patriarchs.

"For God is pleased with those who fear
Him, and who put their hope in His mercy."

But some one will perhaps object what has
been before said, that love is the root of every
other affection. If, then, love does not come
first, how will fear and hope come in? It is
thus: there are two kinds of love. One that
craves for God, and is begotten by the bare
knowledge of His existence. This kind of love
precedes all affections, and even faith itself,
which it fixes in its certainty. Some have
maintained that this love can tend towards
good as its primary object, without any knowledge either going before it or accompanying
it; just as in the orders of the Angels the
seraphim come before the cherubim.

The other love is fervent, extatic, and perfect. This joins the lover with the Beloved,
and is not found till many other affections
have preceded it in the soul, and until the
soul has had her inmost senses cleansed and
healed. This purging from the feverish lan-
guor of the infection of sin nothing can better
effect than the fear of the Lord. For this

fear chases away sin, pierces the carnal affections, neglects nothing, and comforts the blessed mourners. From this fear comes the hope of salvation, and many other gracious blessings, according to Scripture. Theologians divide this fear into three classes; the initial, which dreads punishment; the mercenary, which looks not to lose the reward; and the filial, which is careful not to be parted from the Beloved.

When the soul meditates in fear, she says, with Ezekias, "*I will meditate like a dove.*" The meditation of a dove is a lament, the plaintive song brought on by fear. For this reason perhaps it was that another, king David, says, "*Who will give me the wings as of a dove, and I will flee away, and be at rest?*" It is said fear adds wings to the feet. Let us, then, under the figure of a dove, join meditations of the mixed company of fear and hope. In the Canticles the soul is called by the name of "dove." This dove has two wings, which are fear and hope, and discretion is the tail to serve as a rudder. The wings are silvered with the silver of God's word, and each wing is made up of ten pinions,

ten for faith, ten for hope. Both wings must
be poised equally. The wing of fear must
not sink into despair, nor that of hope be
lifted up to presumption. The left wing is
fear, the right is hope.

The first pinion of the wing of fear is the
severity of God. Of this pinion the instances
of God's severity are the feathers, for example, the fall of the angels, the great deluge,
the ruin of Sodom and Gomorrha, the end of
the traitor Judas, the last judgment when
few are chosen.

The second pinion is everlasting damnation.
The various feathers are the different kinds
of torment: the fire unquenchable, the worm
that dies not, the brimstone, the groans, the
weeping, wailing, and gnashing of teeth, the
cold, the bad companionships, the multitude
of the tormented, the incomprehensible nature
of unending suffering, the absence of hope,
and utter exclusion of the vision of God.

The third pinion is the enormity of sin ;
the feathers are the various kinds of sins, and
their aggravating circumstances.

The fourth pinion is our own frailty; the

feathers are the different particulars in which it shows itself, and the dangers of the future.

The fifth pinion is the seduction of prosperity; the feathers are the perils, through pride and lust, to which we are thus exposed.

The sixth pinion is a crushing adversity, with its feathers of the occasions of impatience, trouble, anger, &c.

The seventh is a domestic foe, with the slippery temptations, for its feathers, of our fleshly nature.

The eighth is the perversity of the devil, and its feathers are his snares and wiles.

The ninth is injustice to the living; its feathers are ingratitude, scandals, &c., against benefactors, neighbours, our own family, and subjects.

The tenth is cruelty to the dead; the feathers are neglect of assistance, so that they remain in torments, and are kept from the enjoyment of glory.

Now for the wing of hope the first pinion is the mercy of God; the feathers are the glory of the Angels, the seeing of Adam, Noe, Lot, David, Peter, Paul, Magdalen, the adulterous woman, the good thief, the prodigal son, etc. Christ is the Saviour. There is also the guardianship of Saints and Angels.

The second pinion is the incomprehensible glory to come ; the feathers being the qualities bestowed on soul and body.

The third pinion is the grace of repentance : the feathers being the various sentiments of contrition, and acts of penance.

The fourth pinion is the sustaining hand of God; the feathers being the various helps He gives, by virtues, gifts, by beatitudes, by the Holy Eucharist, which is so powerful, by penance, and the like.

The fifth is holy joy, with its feathers of prosperity humbly received, and the occasions of doing good thereby.

The sixth is the lesson of sadness, and its feathers are adversities bravely endured.

The seventh is free-will, and its feathers are the modes by which it subjects the flesh.

The eighth is the benevolence of the Saints and Angels, the feathers being their various modes of assistance.

The ninth is the helps of the living, and the feathers are the different ways they assist.

The tenth is the prayers of the dead, how we assist them, and they us.

After the example given, those who wish may have abundant matter of meditation in the whole body of holy Scripture. For wings they may use other affections, as *e.g.*, charity to God and to their neighbour, with meditations inducing to both; on the motives for hating sin and vice. But indeed the meditations on fear lead to the hatred of sin, and many other meditations lead to the love of God and their neighbour.

Let us, then, take to ourselves wings, waking with the dawn, as soon as the morning of the divine light sheds its beams on the earth of the soul; and let us dwell in the uttermost parts of the sea, as on a firm shore of wavering thoughts and boiling desires. Even there the Lord's hand, and not our own industry, shall lead us, and His right hand shall hold us. (*Ps.* cxxxviii.)

We must, however, take care not to let unbelief cut off our wings, or despair break them, or sloth clog them, or avarice bind them, or lust burn them, or gluttony weigh them down.

4

CHAPTER XII.

THE REMOVAL OF IMAGES.

Mystical Theology, or the experimental knowledge of God, is an extatic love, following upon a purely spiritual mode of intelligence, an intelligence not obscured by the clouds of the imagination. One, then, who would give himself to mystical theology, must endeavour after this pure intelligence, otherwise how shall he reach the love that follows on it?

Now, if we examine St. Denys's writings, where he treats of mystical theology, we shall find him laying down a method by which the soul may turn herself from all bodily images, and by which, renouncing all that can be thought, imagined, or understood, the spirit bears itself by love into the divine darkness, where God is known, above all speech, and above all conception of the mind..

St. Denys likens the process to the example of a sculptor making a statue. For the sculptor forms his most beautiful image, whether of wood or stone, simply by removing certain parts of his material. So the spirit, removing by denial whatsoever has imperfection, incompletion, dependency, privation, or changeableness, thus arrives at the idea of God ; God all in act, sovereign, pure, and necessary.

Whether this notion of God be only experimental in the summit of the affections, knit to Him by love ; or whether beyond this experimental knowledge there is a proper, and absolute, though not intuitive intellectual conception of the divine Being, is a matter of dispute amongst the commentators on S. Denys.

If we may abstract and remove all imperfection from Being, the same may be done with power, wisdom, and goodness, and the like. So in the conception of man we may abstract all accidental things, such as motion, posture, figure, &c., and there results a general image or idea of man. But by the abstraction of all privation, dependency, or other imperfections, from being, there results the conception of God, proper and absolute.

Those who reason after this manner add the argument that God Himself answers that this is His Name, saying to Moyses: " Thou shalt say to them, HE WHO IS hath sent me to you." The same affirmation they make concerning the conception of goodness, as Christ in the New Law says: " There is none good but God." S. Augustine seems to lean to this opinion in his treatise on the Holy Trinity, and S. Bonaventura in the sixth *Itinerarium.*

Those that are not learned in metaphysics or theology, may still turn their minds away from images, and seek to go above them and beyond them. In all their meditations and the knowledge they attain of God, they should never stop in that knowledge, but by the force of their affections they should aspire with the gaping mouth of the heart, as it were, to taste the savour of His power, His wisdom, and His goodness, as the attributes of Him who is altogether terrible in His counsels over the sons of men, by the majesty of His power ruling and judging; whose wisdom is great, wonderful, and without end, and who is Himself all sweet, all desirable, loveable exceedingly for His goodness and the torrent of His pleasures.

Now when we are thus reaching out after God, a crowd of troublesome images will rush into the mind, importunately placing themselves before the eyes of the heart. What are we to do? We must wipe them away as well as we can, and cast them outside, shake the hand as it were, and strive to get free of these meshes, and disentangled. Or we may feign not to behold them. Or we may despise them, and go on our way as though they existed not, going through the midst of the turbulent band, and breaking away.

Spiritual thirst should goad us on, so that, as the hart pants for the brooks of water, to escape the heat and the biting of the dogs, so our souls should pant after God. We should be able to say, "My soul desireth Thee, O God. My soul hath thirsted for the strong living God; when shall I come, and appear before the face of God?"

We must know, however, that unless the file of fear has first purged us by an entire and unfeigned repentance, and unless the mind, thus cleared of the rust of sin, shines

clear by reformation in newness of spirit, it
will be vain for us to rise before the light,
striving to reach the height of perfection.
This purgation and illumination are first
necessary. So David says: "Rise after ye
have sat down, ye that eat the bread of
sorrow;" to wit, of that fear without which
no man can be justified before God. For it
were an unmannerly rudeness to offer to kiss
the mouth before having first kissed the feet
with tears, and the hands with thanksgiving.

But the soul, intelligent and cleansed, may
come to such a state as to be little anxious,
whether concerning joys, or pain, or reward.
She has no hard or uneasy thoughts of God,
as a judge who rewards, or who takes vengeance. What she thinks of Him is that He
is all desirable, sweet and mild, most worthy
of being loved, even though He should kill
her. Now when thus love is her only busi-
ness, her only pleasure, let her fly to the embraces of her Bridegroom, and strained to the
Divine Heart by the arms of the most pure
friendship, let her give those chastest kisses
of peace, that peace which passeth all understanding, that so in a torrent of delight, and

of loving devotion, she may say those words
of the spouse, " My Beloved to me, and I
to Him."

RICHARDSON AND SON, PRINTERS, DERBY.

CONTENTS.

OUR LADY'S LIBRARY,

𝔄pprobed by the 𝔅ishop of Nottingham.

The Loves which Reign in the Heart of Mary.
For our Lady's True Lovers, showing how they may increase their love, and live in still closer union with their Mother, by studying the emanations of her Pure Heart. Post 12mo, cloth, blocked black, gold lettering, price 3s.

Mary's Conferences to her Loving Children, both in the World and the Cloister. Bound in cloth, lettered, price 3s. 6d.

Our Lady's Comfort to the Sorrowful. New edition, enlarged and revised. Price 8d.—Cloth gilt, 1s.

A Message from the Mother Heart of Mary. New and enlarged edition. Price 4d.; bound, 6d.

Mary's Call to her Loving Children; or Devotion to the Dying. By the Authoress of the "Path of Mary." Post 12mo, bound in cloth, price 2s. 6d.

Spiritual Exercises of Mary. A Sequel to the "Path of Mary." Royal 32mo, superfine cloth, lettered, price 2s.

The Path of Mary. A new edition, with additions. Approved by the Bishop of Nottingham. Royal 32mo, Price 8d.; bound in cloth, lettered, 1s.

Indulgenced Prayers to be said at Mass, in honour of the Precious Blood. Price 4d. per doz.

Indulgenced Prayers for the Holy Souls and for the Dying. From "Our Lady's Comfort to the Sorrowful." Price 6d. per dozen.

Act of Consecration, and Morning Offering, for those who enter on the Path of Mary. From the "Spiritual Exercises of Mary." Price 1d., or 9d. per dozen.

Efficacious Prayer, known to produce special Graces. Price 1d.; or 9d. per dozen.

Our Lady's Retreat; or Mary's Whispers to her Children during a Nine Days' Retreat.

MINIATURE WORKS OF DEVOTIONAL AND PRACTICAL PIETY.

Demy 18mo, handsome cloth binding, price Sixpence each.

Snares of the Devil. By John Gerson, Chancellor of Paris. With Biographical Sketch.

Seven Gifts of the Holy Ghost. By F. Pergmayer, S.J.

Communion Prayers for Every Day of the Week. By Canon A. C. Arvisenet.

Heavenward. From "Heaven Opened." By Rev. H. Collins.

Comfort for Mourners. By St. Francis de Sales.

Holy Will of God; a Short Rule of Perfection. By Father Benedict Canfield.

Month of Jesus Christ. By Saint Bonaventure.

Stations of the Passion as made in Jerusalem, and Select Devotions on the Passion, from St. Gertrude. Translated by Rev. H. Collins.

The Our Father: Meditations on the Lord's Prayer. By Saint Teresa.

Quiet of the Soul. By Father John de Bonilla. With CURE FOR SCRUPLES. By Dom Schram, O.S.B.

Little Manual of Direction, or Priests, Religious Superiors, &c. By Dom Schram, O.S.B.

Practical Guide to Spiritual Prayer. By John Gerson.

RICHARDSON'S POPULAR CATHOLIC MANUALS.

Mass for the Dead, Dies Iræ, and Prayers for the Faithful Departed. Price 1d.

Sanctification of Sickness; Practical Instructions for the Comfort of the Sick. Price 1d.

Devotions for the Forty Hours' Adoration, or Quarant' Ore; Solemn Exposition; and Benediction of the B. Sacrament. Compiled by a Priest. Price 1d.

Marriage and Family Duties in general. By Archbishop Purcell, of Cincinnati, America. Adapted for English readers by a Priest. Price 1d.

Story of St. Dimas, the "Good Thief." By a Priest. Frontispiece (4th thousand), price 1d.